The Fathering Spirit

E. James Logan

Tulsa, Oklahoma

THE FATHERING SPIRIT
© 2005 by E. James Logan

Published by Insight Publishing Group
8801 S. Yale, Suite 410
Tulsa, OK 74137
918-493-1718

All rights reserved. No part of this book may be reproduced or transmitted in any form or by any means, electronic or mechanical, including photocopying and recording, or by an information storage and retrieval system, without permission in writing from the author.

Unless otherwise noted, Scripture quotations are taken from the King James Version of the Bible. Scripture quotations marked NKJV are taken from the Holy Bible: New King James Version, © 1979, 1980, 1982 by Thomas Nelson, Inc., publishers. Scripture quotations marked NIV are from the New International Version, © 1960, 1962, 1963, 1968, 1971, 1972, 1973, 1975, 1977, 1995 by the Lockman Foundation. Used by permission.

ISBN 1-932503-52-8
Library of Congress catalog card number: 2004118116

Printed in the United States of America

Contents

Foreword

"The Fathering Spirit"

In a day when so many men are looking for their place in life, many have yet to give themselves solely to the plan and purpose of God. They don't know where to go, what to do, or how to do it. One of the primary reasons for this is failure to have a relationship with a father or an individual possessing "a Fathering Spirit."

God is our Father, and the Bible states that He is the one from whom all fatherhood derives its name; in essence, He is the ultimate Father. To reach one's maximum potential, one must put God first. But equally important is the need to establish a relationship with an individual who can assist in fulfilling the plan of God for our lives.

In his book *The Fathering Spirit*, James Logan reveals truths that are necessary for any individual seeking to advance in life. You can't make it alone—and every person, whether male or female, needs to recognize the spiritual leaders in their life as well as the importance of the part that God has ordained them to play.

By reading this book, you will be able to understand why so many areas of your life seem to lack direction and what you can do about it. My prayer is that this book will find its way into the hands of multitudes within the Body of Christ.

I have had the pleasure of working closely in ministry with James Logan, and I have seen firsthand, through his life and by his examples, what God can and will do in the life of an individual who will submit to those in their life who possess "The Fathering Spirit."

Bishop Darrell L. Hines
Founder/Pastor
Christian Faith Fellowship Church, Inc.
Darrell Hines Ministries
Dominion Fellowship Ministries International

Preface

The purpose of this book is to demonstrate the need for the Fathering Spirit to return to the church through scripture and biblical principles.

For years, women have played the dominant role in the Body of Christ. If it were not for women, where would the church be today? We should thank God that women have been faithful to Him and the church; supporting the church prayerfully, financially, and otherwise.

As a result of the absence of the Fathering Spirit in the church, there has also been an absence of strength, an absence of the male presence in the church. The Fathering Spirit ensures that the next generation continues. The Fathering Spirit is what causes the purposes of God to flow continuously from one generation to the next.

The Fathering Spirit is necessary for true apostolic ministry to impact the church. Without the Fathering Spirit, we have a generation that has little or no loyalty, commitment, or service. The Fathering Spirit is what generates and maintains momentum.

Once the Fathering Spirit is released in the church, we will be able to build on each new truth restored—each new move of the Spirit—and finish the work started by those who have the Fathering Spirit.

May we be that generation that finishes what our fathers, the first 12 apostles of Jesus, started. *1 Cor. 3:6 I have planted, Apollos watered; but God gave the increase.* May we be mindful of the words of the Apostle Paul, who had a Fathering Spirit.

2 Tim. 2:1 Thou therefore, my son, be strong in the grace that is in Christ Jesus.

2 Tim. 2:2 And the things that thou hast heard of me among many witnesses, the same commit thou to faithful men, who shall be able to teach others also.

Acknowledgements

I would like to first give all thanks to the Father of my Lord and Savior JesusChrist for giving me the grace to release this book. He truly is the Fathering Spirit!

To my wife and life partner, Deborah, who pastors alongside me and who is the mother of my only two children, Cameron and Llexis. I want to give a special thank you. They have taught me so much about the Fathering Spirit.

To my spiritual parents who birthed me into the gospel, Bishop Darrell and Pastor Pamela Hines, your godly example has been exemplary.

To Bishop Tudor Bismark, Dr. Myles Munroe, Bishop Vaughn McLaughlin, Clifton Sawyer, Dr. Bob Harrison, and Bishop Kenneth Fuller, just to name a few, I would like to thank these as well as others, you all have helped me learn what it truly means to have a Fathering Spirit.

A special thank you to my secretary Alicia Harris and our in-house word processor, Monica Coman, as well as the entire editing staff.

Last, but certainly not least, I want to thank all of Christian Faith Fellowship Church Zion, for allowing me to grow into this revelation as a Fathering Spirit. Thank you so much for your love and support.

Chapter One

What Is Man?

Gen. 1:26 And God said, Let us make man in our image, after our likeness: and let them have dominion over the fish of the sea, and over the fowl of the air, and over the cattle, and over all the earth, and over every creeping thing that creepeth upon the earth.

Gen. 1:27 So God created man in his own image, in the image of God created he him; male and female created he them.

Man was created in the image and likeness of God ('elohim). In Hebrew, 'elohim is a plural word that refers to The Father, The Son, and The Holy Spirit. Therefore, man, created in the image and likeness of God, is a triune being in more than one way. He is a spirit who possesses a soul that lives in a body. He also has within himself the capacity to be a father, son, and a comforting spirit (The Holy Spirit is called "the comforter" in the New Testament).

These, I believe, are three natures that must co-exist in a man who has the true Fathering Spirit. These three natures are nurtured and developed by an earthly father who demonstrates and instills these qualities in his son. Let's look at what God did for man in the beginning to develop his triune nature.

Gen. 1:28 And God blessed them, and God said unto them, Be fruitful, and multiply, and replenish the earth, and subdue it: and have dominion . . . The first words God spoke to man were a blessing. So, man is first blessed. Every man must first know that his Father in heaven blesses him. Adam had no natural earthly father, but his Heavenly Father's first words blessed him. Too often, the first words young boys hear from their fathers are curse words or words that discourage them. Some never hear their father's voice until they're grown and some never hear it at all.

We must understand the first voice a boy hears is the voice that will influence him the most throughout his life. It is the voice that answers the age-old question, the question that every boy asks: Who and what am I?

God answers that question by first pronouncing a blessing upon man and then telling him to be fruitful, to increase on the earth, and to have many sons and daughters whom He will in turn bless. Now man knows his purpose; he now knows he is blessed to increase and cover the earth, conquer it, and rule over it. Adam was blessed by his father and told that he could increase, conquer, and rule (dominate). These are three dominant character traits that God placed in every man.

Fathers show their sons how to increase, conquer, and rule. If the father is not mentally, emotionally, and spiritually healthy, the son will have a warped sense of how and what to increase, conquer, and rule.

The father leaves the son his legacy of what to increase, conquer, and rule over. History shows us the legacy Joseph Kennedy left his sons—President John F., Robert, on down to Ted Kennedy—a legacy of politics and power. Joseph Kennedy taught his sons what to increase, conquer, and dominate. Dr. Martin Luther King did the same thing, and we can see what his sons are increasing, conquering, and ruling over. What are we teaching our sons to increase, conquer, and rule? Is it alcohol, drugs, premarital sex, gambling, a life of crime?

True Godly fathers use our Heavenly Father as the pattern. Let's look at *Gen. 2:7 And the LORD God formed man of the dust of the ground, and breathed into his nostrils the breath of life; and man became a living soul.* Here we see God the Father, our pattern, touching man with His own hands, forming and shaping him.

A Fathering Spirit will not allow anyone else to shape his son; he will not allow the television, movies, video games, or anything else to mold his son. He will do it with his own hands. He won't leave it to chance. He purposely places his hands on his son to shape him into what he desires.

Notice that after He uses His hands, God breathes into His son. God breathes life into Adam, His son. He breathes His own life into His son, His very essence. God puts some of Himself into His son. This is the great investment. How can Adam become anything else but what his Father has given, that he has so much of his Father invested in him. After this the Bible says that the son became a living soul.

Adam was not alive until his Father breathed on him, talked to him, shared his life with him. There are far too many men who are alive but with dead souls. Emotionally empty, drained, or bankrupt because they never had a father to breathe on them, to talk with them, or to pour their lives into them. Consequently, they go through life not knowing their purpose, not knowing they were created to increase, to conquer, and to rule over their circumstances. Instead, they decrease, are defeated, and are ruled by their emotions and dominated to by the world system.

God always blesses His sons. *Gen. 12:1 Now the LORD had said unto Abram, Get thee out of thy country, and from thy kindred, and from thy Father's house, unto a land that I will show thee:*

Gen. 12:2 And I will make of thee a great nation, and I will bless thee, and make thy name great; and thou shalt be a blessing:

Gen. 12:3 And I will bless them that bless thee, and curse him that curseth thee: and in thee shall all families of the earth be blessed.

God told Abram to leave his father and He would bless him, make his name great, and cause him to become a blessing. This is good news, especially for the sons who have no father or whose father left them or they left their fathers. When God becomes our Father, He will bless us beyond what our natural fathers could have done. All we need to do is as Abram did, give God the chance.

Remember, God the Father is the pattern for fathers; He is the great Fathering Spirit. And as we read through scripture, we see God had a better plan for Abram than his natural father, Terah.

The Bible says Terah was an idolator; he worshipped false gods. This was not the legacy God the Father wanted for Abram, so God tells Abram to leave that legacy behind and He would bless him with another one. When God tells us to leave someone behind as important as a father, it's only because He has something better for us. We know that God changed Abram's name to Abraham, blessed him with a son, and he became a great nation. Abraham increased, conquered, and ruled because he followed God. Abraham had a Fathering Spirit.

The proof of Abraham's Fathering Spirit can be heard in the very words of God Himself: *Gen. 18:17 And the LORD said, Shall I hide from Abraham that thing which I do; Gen. 18:18 Seeing that Abraham shall surely become a great and mighty nation, and all the nations of the earth shall be blessed in him?*

Gen. 18:19 For I know him, that he will command his children and his household after him, and they shall keep the way of the LORD, to do justice and judgment; that the LORD may bring upon Abraham that which he hath spoken of him.

God was able to do what He promised Abraham because Abraham had a Fathering Spirit. Abraham would not cease to teach his children the ways of the true and living God. Abraham ruled his house well and God increased him. God knew Abraham would do what was necessary to raise his son Isaac in the ways of the Lord. *Gen. 21:10 Wherefore she said unto Abraham, Cast out this bondwoman and her son: for the son of this bondwoman shall not be heir with my son, even with Isaac. Gen. 21:11 And the thing was very grievous in Abraham's sight because of his son.*

Abraham had to remove the slave mentality from his household if Isaac was to become all that God intended. It meant releasing his illegitimate son so the legacy would continue in the one God chose. This was painful for Abraham, but he had a Fathering Spirit and had to obey God. Abraham also had to be willing to release Isaac if he was going to fulfill God's purpose in the earth. Sometimes fathers have difficulty releasing their children. This hinders and can even stop the plan of God. The Fathering Spirit is one who understands that his son is not only his own son; he is a son of God too.

Gen. 22:1 And it came to pass after these things, that God did tempt Abraham, and said unto him, Abraham: and he said, Behold, here I am.

Gen. 22:2 And he said, Take now thy son, thine only son Isaac, whom thou lovest, and get thee into the land of Moriah; and offer him there for a burnt offering upon one of the mountains which I will tell thee of.

Gen. 22:7 And Isaac spake unto Abraham his father, and said, My father: and he said, Here am I, my son. And he said, Behold the fire and the wood: but where is the lamb for a burnt offering?

Gen. 22:8 And Abraham said, My son, God will provide himself a lamb for a burnt offering: so they went both of them together.

Gen. 22:9 And they came to the place which God had told him of; and Abraham built an altar there, and laid the wood in order, and bound Isaac his son, and laid him on the altar upon the wood.

Gen. 22:10 And Abraham stretched forth his hand, and took the knife to slay his son.

As difficult as it was, Abraham obeyed God and was willing to totally release his son into God's hand. Abraham took his knife and stretched forth his hand—the hand he used to shape Isaac, the same hand he used to mold Isaac, he now stretched it forth to release him. We must be willing to take our hand—the same hand we used to play catch with our sons, to teach them to read, to study, and to pray—and use it to release them into the hands of God.

Oh what a lesson of faith Abraham taught Isaac; not only do I trust God but I also trust you in His hand. Those with the Fathering Spirit know how to trust their sons in the hand of God. They may not see all of what God has in mind, but they commend them to God.

Acts 20:32 And now, brethren, I commend you to God, and to the word of his grace, which is able to build you up, and to give you an inheritance among all them which are sanctified.

These are the words of the Apostle Paul as he was about to reach his final destination. Fathers with the true Fathering Spirit know how to commend their sons to God and the word of His grace that we might be built up and receive our inheritance. (Isaac would not have seen his father's faith and been built up had Abraham not been willing to release him to God.) The Fathering Spirits in our lives realize that God has a plan for our lives as well as their own, and they want us to receive our Godly inheritance. They lovingly release us into the hands of God and His grace.

Abraham was a Fathering Spirit, he believed what the Lord told him years ago, and he never deviated from the word of the lord concerning his son Isaac. Even after Abraham was much older, he protected his son's legacy.

Gen. 25:5-6 And Abraham gave all that he had unto Isaac. But unto the sons of the concubines, which Abraham had, Abraham gave gifts, and sent them away from Isaac his son, while he yet lived, eastward, unto the east country.

Abraham was not afraid to remove or send away any hindrances in Isaac's life, anything that would compete with God's plan for his life. Abraham gave his other children gifts, but he never gave them what God promised Isaac. Abraham fathered all of his children, but Isaac was his legacy; Isaac was God's choice through which the world would be blessed.

Gen. 25:11 And it came to pass after the death of Abraham, that God blessed his son Isaac; and Isaac dwelt by the well Lahairoi. Now that Abraham was dead, God blessed Isaac. God adopted Isaac, so Isaac needed to have a personal relationship with God the Father if God was going to do all He had promised his father Abraham.

Spiritual sons must come to the place in their lives where they hear God's voice for themselves. They must hear God's blessing for their lives personally. A son cannot live off what his father always told him about God; he must learn it for himself if he is going to increase, conquer, and rule well. In God's talks with Isaac, God begins shaping and molding Isaac as He had done to his father Abraham. Sons must build on the legacy left them by their fathers.

Gen. 26:1 And there was a famine in the land, beside the first famine that was in the days of Abraham. And Isaac went unto Abimelech king of the Philistines unto Gerar.

Gen. 26:2 And the LORD appeared unto him and said, Go not down into Egypt; dwell in the land which I shall tell thee of:

Gen. 26:3 Sojourn in this land, and I will be with thee, and will bless thee; for unto thee, and unto thy seed, I will give all these countries, and I will perform the oath which I sware unto Abraham thy father;

Gen. 26:4 And I will make thy seed to multiply as the stars of heaven, and will give unto thy seed all these countries; and in thy seed shall all the nations of the earth be blessed;

Gen. 26:5 Because that Abraham obeyed my voice, and kept my charge, my commandments, my statutes, and my laws.

Gen. 26:6 And Isaac dwelt in Gerar:

Gen. 26:12 Then Isaac sowed in that land, and received in the same year an hundredfold: and the LORD blessed him.

Gen. 26:13 And the man waxed great, and went forward, and grew until he became very great:

Gen. 26:14 For he had possession of flocks, and possession of herds, and great store of servants: and the Philistines envied him.

Isaac increased, conquered, and ruled because he followed in the footsteps of his father Abraham who followed God. *Gen. 26:18 And Isaac digged again the wells of water, which they had digged in the days of Abraham his father . . .*

The Fathering Spirit will always leave landmarks that his son can follow during difficult times. The son will easily remember what his father did during a drought or a storm and draw from that in order to navigate through his own storms. One of the ways the Fathering Spirit leaves an inheritance for his sons is by teaching them how to handle the storms of life. Paul said this to the church at Corinth: *2 Cor. 12:14 Behold, the third time I am ready to come to you; and I will not be burdensome to you: for I seek not yours, but you: for the children ought not to lay up for the parents, but the parents for the children.* Paul says, I have prepared myself to come to you so when I arrive you won't be burdened by my coming. As a matter of fact, when I come, I'm bringing something to leave with you, because the father should store up to provide for his children, not the children for the fathers.

I believe this is also what is meant in Luke 1:17 and Mal. 4:6 *And he shall turn the heart of the fathers to the children, and the heart of the children to their fathers, lest I come and smite the earth with a curse.* Those who have the Fathering Spirit will store up for their children. They will not build monuments to themselves. They will build to leave and store up for the next generation. Their concern is not self, but the children. When the children of this generation see and know the fathers of this generation care and are storing up for them, they will turn their hearts back to them. They will turn and give respect, love, and their allegiance back to their fathers.

Once the Fathering Spirit is released back into the church, the generational blessings that began with God to Adam in the garden of Eden will flow down to this generation, who rule and reign through Christ Jesus.

Paul says in *Col. 3:21 Fathers, provoke not your children to anger, lest they be discouraged.* The Fathering Spirit challenges without discouraging, demands without damaging, and stresses without striving.

Prov. 17:6b . . . the glory of children are their fathers. The Fathering Spirit brings and deposits glory on the next generation. The reason so many children have low self-esteem, low self-worth, rob, steal, rape, and kill with little or no remorse is because they have no fathers. They have lost their glory, their strength to resist, and their reason for living, caring, or giving.

They walk around almost aimlessly without purpose or destiny because there are no *true* fathers in their lives. When a child has a godly father, they carry themselves differently; there is a sense of confidence in their stride. They do better in school, are able to make better decisions, and are less likely to be negatively affected by peer pressure because their *father* is their glory, not a gang or drugs. They have healthier attitudes toward professional athletes and entertainers because their *father* is their glory. Without the father in place, children inevitably look for their glory somewhere else. God only knows where these places are. Statistics tell us of some of these places, but I dare say some of them we have yet to discover.

The Fathering Spirit is what is going to help turn the tide in our communities, our nation, and even the world. It's the Fathering Spirit that is going to help usher in the last wave of God's glory back to the church. The glory always departs when fathers are absent. *1 Sam. 4:21 And she named the child Ichabod, saying, The glory is departed from Israel: because the ark of God was taken, and because of her father in law and her husband.* She named her child Ichabod because Israel lost the Ark and because she lost her father-in-law and the father of her child. Surely, the glory is gone from her life with the absence of her heavenly and earthly coverings.

The New Testament makes it clear that the glory of a woman is her hair because she uses her hair as a covering or a veil. Long hair symbolizes being covered by the Heavenly Father and an earthly father. *1 Cor. 11:15 But if a woman have long hair, it is a glory to her: for her hair is given her for a covering.*

Women who grow up in homes without fathers or women who raise children without husbands are exposed, uncovered, and without the glory they need.

Num. 27:6 And the LORD spake unto Moses, saying,

Num. 27:7 The daughters of Zelophehad speak right: thou shalt surely give them a possession of an inheritance among their father's brethren; and thou shalt cause the inheritance of their father to pass unto them.

Num. 27:8 And thou shalt speak unto the children of Israel, saying, If a man die, and have no son, then ye shall cause his inheritance to pass unto his daughter.

Prov. 13:22 A good man leaveth an inheritance to his children's children: and the wealth of the sinner is laid up for the just.

Notice that it is the *good man* who leaves an inheritance for his children's children. Only a male can be the *his* and only a *father* can have children. So we can safely interpret this scripture this way: *"a good father leaves an inheritance for his children's children."* And scripture says not just for the sons, but for the daughters as well.

One reason divorce is so high is because fathers are not leaving an inheritance of love, commitment, and stability for their daughters. Instead, young girls are being sexually and verbally abused, leaving them an inheritance of emotional scars and psychological dysfunction that remains into marriage.

When a father dies and leaves his daughters without an inheritance, they must find ways of support which often involves compromising themselves after which they lose self-esteem and respect for the male gender. In biblical times daughters were not equipped to farm land and since they had no inheritance, they had to sell themselves as slaves or become prostitutes just to survive. Ruth had to go and glean in the fields for leftovers.

Gen. 31:14 And Rachel and Leah answered and said unto him, Is there yet any portion or inheritance for us in our father's house?

The Fathering Spirit is as important for the female as it is for the male. When girls are forced to grow up without their father guarding, protecting, and nurturing them, they grow up without knowing the gentle touch of a man. They are not exposed to nor can they know that the strength of a man is to be used to guard, protect, and assist her and not to beat, abuse, or control her.

In 1 Chron. 6 the lineage of the sons of the priests are mentioned, but the names of Eli, Hophni, and Phinehas are not mentioned and neither is Ichabod. When the Fathering Spirit is absent, the priesthood is vacant; and when there are no priests, there is a curse for there is no one to minister to God on behalf of families.

Hosea 4:6 My people are destroyed for lack of knowledge: because thou hast rejected knowledge, I will also reject thee, that thou shalt be no priest to me: seeing thou hast forgotten the law of thy God, I will also forget thy children.

The chain of command in the kingdom of God is this: *Dan. 9:6 Neither have we hearkened unto thy servants the **prophets**, which spake in thy name to our K**ings** our **princes*** (priests) *and our **fathers**, and to **all the people** of the land.*

Notice that prophets speak to the kings. The prophet heard directly from God, not the king. The king was to hear from the prophet what thus saith the Lord. This is what maintained the government of God in Israel. When the prophets stop speaking or the kings stop hearing, the chain of command is broken, the princes are confused, and the fathers decline.

1 Cor. 4:15 For though ye have ten thousand instructors in Christ, yet have ye not many fathers: for in Christ Jesus I have begotten you through the gospel.

1 Cor. 4:16 Wherefore I beseech you, be ye followers of me.

1 Cor. 4:17 For this cause have I sent unto you Timotheus, who is my beloved son, and faithful in the Lord, who shall bring you into remembrance of my ways which be in Christ, as I teach everywhere in every church.

Paul says we may have ten thousand instructors but not many (or a few) spiritual fathers. He goes on to say, "I have begotten you through the gospel. In other words, you were born again through my preaching. Since you were birthed into the kingdom by me, continue following me! Why would you follow another?"

Under normal circumstances, we are not born into this world and raised up by another man other than our father. Paul says this is not normal, especially since he is willing and available. Spiritual fathers are to be the example by which spiritual sons pattern themselves. Timothy should have been a great spiritual father because of the example of the Apostle Paul.

The Fathering Spirit is crucial to the development of every leadership position in the world and especially in the kingdom of God. If the Fathering Spirit does not return to the church, we are destined to repeat what Israel perpetually practiced; never leaving a succession plan that ensures that sons are nurtured and developed to replace their fathers as leaders.

When God makes promises to the fathers, He cuts a covenant with them. When the fathers are absent, there is no covenant.

Deu. 7:8 But because the LORD loved you, and because he would keep the oath which he had sworn unto your fathers, hath the

LORD brought you out with a mighty hand, and redeemed you out of the house of bondmen, from the hand of Pharaoh king of Egypt.

Mal. 4:5 Behold, I will send you Elijah the prophet before the coming of the great and dreadful day of the LORD:

Mal. 4:6 And he shall turn the heart of the fathers to the children, and the heart of the children to their fathers, lest I come and smite the earth with a curse.

Luke 1:17 And he shall go before him in the spirit and power of Elias, to turn the hearts of the fathers to the children, and the disobedient to the wisdom of the just; to make ready a people prepared for the Lord.

It's the Fathering Spirit's operation in the church that will prepare a people for the coming of the Lord. The Fathering Spirit teaches the children about the covenant they have with their God. The fathers teach the children how to pray, believe God, and fight the good fight of faith.

Paul told and showed Timothy, his spiritual son, how to fight the good fight of faith, *2 Tim. 4:7 I have fought a good fight, I have finished my course, I have kept the faith.* This is what the Fathering Spirit does; it prepares the next generation. It demonstrates the will of God through teaching and living the covenant and inheriting the promises. When the Fathering Spirit is absent, the next generation is confused and frustrated because they see no way of accomplishing their dreams. They see no one demonstrating for them how to walk in the covenant promises of God. As a result, they see churches as nothing but social clubs where people come to meet and have a religious experience without coming into intimate relations with the Lord Jesus Christ. For them there is no reason to attend church or live a Christian life. In their eyes, there is no inheritance worth having or faith worth fighting for.

Jude 1:3b . . . exhort you that ye should earnestly contend for the faith which was once delivered unto the saints. One cannot fight for what has not been passed down to them. Remember, the father is the one who leaves the inheritance.

Growing up as a young man without a father figure in my life, I looked for who I was in other men—some famous, some in the church, and some in the community I lived in. This created confusion because I was trying to fuse together several different personalities into my own.

If I liked how a certain man dressed, I would attempt to dress like him. If I liked how a certain man walked, I would walk like him. If I liked how another man combed his hair, I combed mine that same way. I ran the football like Gale Sayers and played basketball like Walt Frazier. I was so many people, I didn't know *I* was somebody. I was living my life through other people who had not left me an inheritance. They left me wonderful memories but nothing I could put on an application or résumé for a job. They left me with great childhood stories but nothing I could use in my marriage or in raising my children.

I found myself mixed up, confused, and with very few skills to deal with life's real issues. Consequently, I would pretend nothing was wrong or act like nothing bothered me. If a relationship went wrong (usually because of me), I would just move on to the next one. If I lost a job, no problem, I'll just move on the next one—never getting my issues dealt with because I didn't know I had any. This continued into my early adulthood, and didn't end until I allowed God the Father to show me who I was through the Word of God, the Spirit of God, and of course, through my spiritual parents.

Without true fathers, we do not know who we are, what we like, or what our assignment truly is and we become desperate to achieve and accomplish anything. We become people pleasers; looking for affirmation anywhere we can get it. We are fertile ground for the enemy to place strongholds in our lives that get stronger and stronger unless we allow the Holy Spirit to deal with them. Strongholds manifest on the streets in gangs, in night clubs/sports bars with our friends, or in going from partner to partner trying to find our identity and someone to affirm us.

Make no mistake about it, everyone is being fathered. The question is, *who* is fathering you? Jesus said in *John 8:44 Ye are of your father the devil, and the lusts of your father ye will do.*

We all are doing the desires of the one who is fathering us at this very moment. If you want to know who your father is, check out your actions and attitudes. We are all doing just as Jesus said in John 8:44. We've all heard the saying "like father, like son." It's true; it's a biblical principle. *John 5:19 Then answered Jesus and said unto them, Verily, verily, I say unto you, The Son can do nothing of himself, but what he seeth the Father do: for what things soever he doeth, these also doeth the Son likewise.*

Sons do what they see their fathers doing; we can't help it. Like father—like son, like son—like father. It's vitally important to know who your father is so you don't go through life imitating the wrong man, living in a fantasy world where you think less of yourself than who you truly are and what you can accomplish.

The Apostle Paul is constantly writing to the church encouraging them to be imitators (followers) of his ways. *1 Cor. 4:16 Wherefore I beseech you, be ye followers of me.*

1 Cor. 4:17 For this cause have I sent unto you Timotheus, who is my beloved son, and faithful in the Lord, who shall bring you into remembrance of my ways which be in Christ, as I teach every where in every church.

Paul sent his son Timothy so they could see how he lived *through* Timothy. Because true sons always do what their fathers do, they have their fathers' ways. Their father can be seen in how they live, pray, teach, and conduct business.

Fathers don't have to go everywhere themselves because they can send sons in their places. Their sons will do what they would do, say what they would say, and accomplish what they would accomplish. This is why every leader needs to have true sons in order to accomplish more than they could possibly accomplish by themselves. The cry of every pastor is, "Give me true sons so I can finish the work God has called me to."

It's discouraging and disheartening for a father to see his sons doing something other than what he himself is doing. If the father is succeeding, he wonders why his sons are failing. If the father is advancing, he wonders why his sons are retreating. The same holds true in the reverse; if the father is not beating his children, he wonders where his sons picked up the idea of beating their children. If the father is not mishandling his affairs, he wonders why his son's affairs are not in order. He wonders where they learned this behavior.

This may be a sign that they are not true sons, because their actions are those of another man. Their behavior patterns are those of another man. Someone else is their father. They lived under his roof, ate his food, and wore the clothes he bought for them, but they aren't his sons. They took his name, but someone else fathered them, someone else conceived them.

1 Cor. 4:15 For though ye have ten thousand instructors in Christ, yet have ye not many fathers: for in Christ Jesus I have begotten (conceived) *you through the gospel.*

Gal. 4:19 My dear children, for whom I am again in the pains of childbirth until Christ is formed in you . . . NIV

Those with the Fathering Spirit can see the potential in their sons and, by the power of the Holy Spirit, bring about a change in their lives. The father has the God-given ability to literally change the destiny of their sons.

Prov. 1:8 My son, hear the instruction of thy father . . . The son must learn to receive instruction, correction, and discipline from his father *Prov. 1:9 For they shall be an ornament of grace unto thy head, and chains about thy neck.* Listening to our fathers brings grace into our lives.

Prov. 2:1 My son, if thou wilt receive my words, and hide my commandments with thee;

Prov. 2:2 So that thou incline thine ear unto wisdom, and apply thine heart to understanding;

Prov. 2:5 Then shalt thou understand the fear of the LORD, and find the knowledge of God.

The Fathering Spirit is strong enough to alter the course of a son's life. Rachel, dying while giving birth to her son, named him Benoni, which means "son of sorrow" or "son of my mourning." After her death, his father, Jacob, changed his named to Benjamin, which means "son of my strength" or "son of my right hand." Benjamin could have grown up with the stigma over him that his life brought death and sorrow to his mother. Can you imagine how a child would feel growing up thinking he or she caused their own mother so much pain that she eventually died. Think of the dejection and rejection a child would have. They might think that the rest of the family blamed them for their mother's death. The psychological implications are enormous. But the Fathering Spirit in Jacob quickly went into action and he renamed his son.

In the Hebrew culture at that time, the name carried with it the nature, character, and future of the person. Jacob quickly changed his son's name, thereby altering the course of his life. Instead of Benoni growing up with the stigma of death and sorrow over his head, Benjamin grows up believing in himself as his father's right hand. Instead of growing up as a sorry individual, he grows up as a strong individual with strength of character and the love of his father and brothers. All because the Fathering Spirit refused to let a mother's pain be his son's destruction.

Saul, one of Benjamin's ten sons, became Israel's first king. The most famous Benjamite was also named Saul. He became the author of two-thirds of the New Testament. Like his forefather Benjamin, his name was also changed, from Saul to Paul.

Chapter Two

The Seed

Gen. 26:24 And the LORD appeared unto him the same night and said, I am the God of Abraham thy father: fear not, for I am with thee, and will bless thee, and multiply thy seed for my servant Abraham's sake.

Notice God never calls Himself the God of thy mother. Seed does not come from the mother, it comes from the father. God is the first father. He is called the father of glory in Eph. 1:17.

The word "father" is an interesting word. The father is the founder of a family, he who begets a child, a male parent. A father is an originator (the one who comes first), a teacher, one who exercises paternal care over another. Just as there are absentee fathers in homes all over the world, there are absentee fathers in churches across the globe. The father carries the seed; he is the seed giver. The fruit is determined by the seed, so consequently the results we get in life are determined by whose seed we received and reproduced.

When the father is absent—whether through death or dysfunction—or present without performing his fatherly duties, the enemy of mankind gladly steps in and presents ***his*** seed for the purpose of reproducing himself in the earth.

Let's look at the first opportunity satan took to sow his evil seed in the earth. *Gen. 3:1 Now the serpent was more subtle than any beast of the field which the LORD God had made. And he said unto the woman, Yea, hath God said, Ye shall not eat of every tree of the garden?*

Notice that the serpent *said.* He spoke a word to the woman called Eve. This may seem like an insignificant thing, but I assure you it's not. Words are very powerful. As a matter of fact, scripture says **words** are seeds. *Mark 4:14 The sower soweth the word.* Satan, knowing that words are seeds, begins his discourse with Eve, sowing his seed.

Where was Adam? Why would he allow satan to sow seed into her heart this way? Adam was a type of father to Eve. Remember, God caused a deep sleep to come on Adam and took Eve out of his side. Remember our definition. Adam was first; he was the originator; he was a father with a Fathering Spirit.

He could have called Eve over to the side and said, "Hey, don't listen to this guy. Remember the words God the Father said (that I repeated to you)." However, Adam was present without performing. He did not perform his fatherly duties and speak into the situation; consequently, Eve fell into sin and he along with her. When the father fails to perform his fatherly duties, the whole family suffers. Fathers have authority in their homes and with authority comes responsibility. Responsibility is *the ability to respond* to a situation. Adam had the God-given ability to respond, but he didn't. How many fathers, pastors, teachers, and educators have the ability to respond but never do? This attitude was birthed through Adam—the first father—and many have not broken its hold on their lives.

Allow me to say that the Fathering Spirit is not a male domination tactic, nor is it a suggestion to return to the years when women were in complete subservience to men. This is not what I'm saying. Women are shortening the gap in their quest for equal relevance in the world today, which is as it should be. Nevertheless, the Fathering Spirit must not be lost or ignored in the process. The Fathering Spirit is necessary in business where mentors can instill courage, competence, integrity, and commitment into the lives of those climbing the corporate ladder.

The Fathering Spirit demands responsibility. It demands that an issue be addressed because of its lasting effects on the following generations. Without the return of the Fathering Spirit, we will continue as Adam did in the Garden of Eden, ignoring real problems and not addressing current situations. The situation in the garden was one of power and upward mobility. Eve wanted to be like God. She wanted more power, more upward mobility. She felt held back, stifled, and possibly unappreciated.

No one can encourage you like your father can. No one can make you feel valued like your father. After losing an important ball game and everybody is down in the dumps, a father is the only one who can bring that child out of depression. Their words reach deep into the hearts of their children and pull them back up to a place of importance and significance. The Fathering Spirit has power for change!

When Adam failed to respond, we know that things got worse. As a matter of fact, they got so bad that God the Father had to intervene. After Adam failed to respond, God went looking for him and asked where he was. *Gen. 3:9 And the LORD God called unto Adam, and said unto him, Where art thou*? God was looking for the one who was responsible. He was not looking for Eve because He never spoke directly to Eve about the fruit; He spoke to Adam. God went looking for the one He left in charge, the one who had the Fathering Spirit, the one who had the power to change the situation—He went looking for Adam.

Notice what Adam says in *Gen. 3:12 And the man said, The woman whom thou gavest to be with me, she gave me of the tree, and I did eat.* The word gave here in Hebrew means to "set in place, to appoint." You see, Eve was not the one who was supposed to "set things in place" or establish order. That was Adam's job—not because he was a man, but because God spoke to him first. Adam was created first, then Eve. This is God's order. Adam was supposed to set the order as it was given to him by God. Since he failed, present without performing, Eve set the wrong order. The Fathering Spirit sets things in place, establishes order, appoints direction and purpose—not his own, but God's. This is God's way.

Gen. 2:24 Therefore shall a man leave his father and his mother, and shall cleave unto his wife: and they shall be one flesh. Notice that Adam says a man must leave his father **and** his mother. This is not just talking about family. He is stating the order, (first) leaving his father and (secondly) his mother. The father must have something to say about his son's leaving; this is the Fathering Spirit. It is a spiritual principle that is to work for the home as well as the church. Think about it. Even during intercourse, you and I (if not in vitro) first left the father as sperm, entered the mother's womb, impregnated her, and after nine months left our mother to enter the world. This is God's way.

The Fathering Spirit is a nurturing spirit that sets things in place and establishes order. Where there is order, there cannot be chaos. Order is the methodical arrangement of things, established succession, and the proper state or condition of things. (Webster's Columbia Reference Dictionary)

For anything to be methodical, someone must have established the method. And in order for a thing to be established, someone must establish it. So for the Christian, God creates the method, establishes the succession, and sets the proper state and conditions.

God is Father. He is first. All things came out of Him. He created all things; God is the ultimate Fathering Spirit. The writer of the book of Hebrews says, *Furthermore we have had fathers of our flesh which corrected us, and we gave them reverence: shall we not much rather be in subjection unto the Father of spirits, and live? Heb. 12:9*

God is spirit. He is the Fathering Spirit. He created us in His own image and likeness. (Gen. 1:26) God created us to be like Him. So, what did He do when Adam was present without performing? He scolded him and He judged him, but He also covered him. After God passed sentence on Adam and Eve He did an amazing thing, He fathered them! He loved them, nurtured them, and covered them. *Gen. 3:21 Unto Adam also and to his wife did the LORD God make coats of skins, and clothed them.* The Fathering Spirit never exposes; he always covers. If he exposes, he does it to the people involved, not the world. And afterward, he covers just as the Lord did.

Try hard not to reprimand your children in public; it humiliates them. But if you cover them in public love and encourage them, you will build them up. This is the Fathering Spirit.

We cannot hope to love like this without God the Father. Without His Holy Spirit living inside of us, the best we could hope for is to duplicate what our earthly fathers did to us. And the reality is, too much of what was placed upon us was pressure, stress, ungodly expectations, neglect, and sometimes abuse. The true Fathering Spirit brings love, comfort, liberty, and growth; even during difficult times. *Gen. 22:1 And it came to pass after these things, that God did tempt Abraham, and said unto him, Abraham: and he said, Behold, here I am.*

Gen. 22:2 And he said, Take now thy son, thine only son Isaac, whom thou lovest, and get thee into the land of Moriah; and offer him there for a burnt offering upon one of the mountains which I will tell thee of.

Gen. 22:7 And Isaac spake unto Abraham his father, and said, My father: and he said Here am I, my son. And he said, Behold the fire and the wood: but where is the lamb for a burnt offering?

Gen. 22:8 And Abraham said, My son, God will provide himself a lamb for a burnt offering: so they went both of them together.

Abraham provided comfort for his son, whom he was prepared to kill on an altar made with his own hands. Abraham was an awesome father. He showed his son how the Lord always provides. Even when he didn't know all the answers, he still demonstrated faith to his son.

Gen. 22:9 And they came to the place which God had told him of; and Abraham built an altar there, and laid the wood in order, and bound Isaac his son, and laid him on the altar upon the wood.

Gen. 22:10 And Abraham stretched forth his hand, and took the knife to slay his son.

Gen. 22:11 And the angel of the LORD called unto him out of heaven, and said, Abraham, Abraham: and he said, Here am I.

Gen. 22:12 And he said, Lay not thine hand upon the lad, neither do thou any thing unto him: for now I know that thou fearest God, seeing thou hast not withheld thy son, thine only son from me.

How many fathers (natural and spiritual) are demonstrating this kind of faith in difficult situations to their sons? The Fathering Spirit is one of faith, one of great faith in the midst of impossible odds. The Fathering Spirit demonstrates faith to their sons, a faith that works by love (Gal. 5:6). The God we serve is based on whose seed was sown into our hearts. If our father was an alcoholic, the seeds of alcoholism will be in the children and they will have a greater chance of becoming or serving that same god.

The Bible mentions the phrases "The God of Abraham, Isaac, and Jacob" ten times in the Old Testament; "The God of thy father(s)" once; and "The God of thy father" five times. The Bible mentions the phrases "The God of thy Mothers Sarah, Rebekah, and Rachel" zero times; "The God of Sarah" zero times, and "The God of thy mother" zero times. It is clear that God has a special place for fathers and fatherhood in scripture and in the life of the believer.

The first mention of the word father is in *Gen. 2:24: Therefore shall a man leave his father and his mother, and shall cleave unto his wife: and they shall be one flesh.*

The word "father" in Hebrew means the founder of the household, originator, producer, and generator. Father is a position of high honor; therefore, the name father carries high honors.

God said in the very beginning that a man would leave his father and mother and cleave to his wife and they shall become one flesh. When a man leaves his father and mother, he has left in God's order. When a man leaves just his mother, he has left home without the honor of his father spoken over his life.

In Gen. 49, Jacob called all of his sons together before he died and spoke over and into their lives. He told them who they were and what they were capable of doing. Solomon, one of Jacob's sons, was the richest and wisest man who ever lived. If we could attain just a portion of Solomon's wisdom, we could do wonders in this world.

Prov. 1:8 My son, hear the instruction of thy father, and forsake not the law of thy mother: These were the words of the wisest man who ever lived. Why did he say it? Because this is what made him so wise. Listening to and obeying the instructions of his godly father. The Hebrew word for "instruction" here means *discipline,* but this discipline teaches children *how* to live a godly life and in the fear of the Lord. When the father is absent from the home, it is almost impossible for children to learn proper discipline and the fear of the Lord.

As a result, we now have a society of people who lack discipline and self-control. They find it impossible to resist temptation and the desire to satisfy flesh. Whatever flesh wants, flesh gets! They get pregnant, do drugs, and skip school. Then, when you ask them why, they say they don't know; they just felt like it; they couldn't help themselves. The phrase *law of thy mother* that Solomon talks about is the Hebrew word *torah.* This means *direction* and *instruction.* So, children receive *warning, discipline, and chastisement* from their father and *law, instruction,* and *guidelines* from their mother.

With single-parent households accounting for 27 percent of all family households, we have a society of people with *instruction* without *warning; knowledge* without *wisdom; information* without *revelation; opportunity* without *discipline; action* without the thought of *consequence;* and *punishment* without *chastisement.* This is why God says in the last days that the spirit of Elijah (the Fathering Spirit) will ***return*** to the earth to (Luke 1:17) . . . *turn the hearts of the fathers to the children, and the disobedient to the wisdom of the just; to make ready a people prepared for the Lord.* It literally means that the Fathering Spirit will change the attitudes of the fathers toward their children, and make the unpersuadable and disagreeable desire the wisdom of God.

We must be people who not only have instruction, but also have the discipline to carry it out. The church isn't ready for Christ's return, because we have too many people with the mothering spirit and too many people accustomed to being mothered. Too many people wanting pastors to *nurture* them rather than *discipline* them.

Elijah did not play with Israel; he came on the scene saying if God be God, then serve Him and stop being passive and double-minded. How long will you halt between two opinions? Get some discipline, some strength, and some backbone in your life and serve the one you know is God. Jesus will come back when the Fathering Spirit returns to the church.

1 Kings 18:36 And it came to pass at the time of the offering of the evening sacrifice, that Elijah the prophet came near, and said, LORD God of Abraham, Isaac, and of Israel, let it be known this day that thou art God in Israel, and that I am thy servant, and that I have done all these things at thy word.

1 Kings 18:37 Hear me, O LORD, hear me, that this people may know that thou art the LORD God, and that thou hast turned their heart back again.

Notice what happens after the hearts of the fathers are turned back to God.

1 Kings 18:38 Then the fire of the LORD fell . . . 1 Kings 18:39 And when ***all the people saw it****, they fell on their faces: and they said, The LORD, he is the God;*

All the people will acknowledge God as Father when the Fathering Spirit is released.

1 Pet. 3:7 Likewise, ye husbands, dwell with them according to knowledge, giving honour unto the wife, as unto the weaker vessel . . .

If a woman after marrying (now a wife) is stronger than she has ever been in every way yet the Bible calls her the "weaker vessel," how much weaker is a ***single*** mother without a father in the home.

Heb. 12:6 For whom the Lord loveth he chasteneth, (disciplines) *and scourgeth every son whom he receiveth.* Scourging was an act of punishment whereby the recipient received 39 stripes—13 on the bare chest and 13 upon each shoulder. The Father is the one who puts the stripes on his son's back when he needs a whipping. We have too many sons who won't take a whipping from their fathers and too many fathers who are afraid to whip their sons.

As the world is redefining what ***real*** child abuse is and good godly parents are fearful of whipping their children, so is the church in the spiritual sense. *1 Cor. 15:46 Howbeit that was not first which is spiritual, but that which is natural; and afterward that which is spiritual.* Healthy sons will show evidence of whipping in their lives. Whether there are scars to prove it or a disciplined life, there will be evidence.

Sons without scars are dangerous to themselves and to others, having not understood or gone through the cost nor paid the price through chastisement.

Heb. 12:7 If ye endure chastening, (discipline and correction) *God dealeth with you as with sons; for what son is he whom the father chasteneth not?*

Heb. 12:8 But if ye be without chastisement, whereof all are partakers, then are ye bastards (the Greek word "*nothos*" means illegitimate), *and not sons.*

Heb. 12:9 Furthermore, we have had fathers of our flesh which corrected us, and we gave them (respect) *reverence: shall we not much rather be in* (submission) *subjection unto the Father of spirits, and live?*

Heb. 12:10 GWT Our fathers on earth disciplined us for a short time in the way they thought was best. But God disciplines us to help us, so we can become holy as he is.

Heb. 12:11 We do not enjoy being disciplined. It is painful, but later, after we have learned from it, we have peace, because we start living in the right way.

Heb. 12:11 NIV No discipline seems pleasant at the time, but painful. Later on, however, it produces a harvest of righteousness and peace for those who have been trained by it.

Here it is stated that those who have not been chastised and disciplined cannot produce fruits of righteousness and peace. This means that those who come out of their loins are not righteous and not at peace with themselves or others. This creates confusion, church splits, and sons leaving prematurely or being frustrated and contaminating others. An undisciplined son is a disgrace to his father and mother. *Prov. 17:25 A foolish son is a grief to his father, and bitterness to her that bare him. Prov. 10:1 The proverbs of Solomon. A wise son maketh a glad father: but a foolish son is the heaviness of his mother.* Solomon had many foolish brothers who were either not disciplined or refused the instruction and discipline of their fathers.

Heb. 12:12 NIV Therefore, strengthen your feeble arms and weak knees.

Heb. 12:13 "Make level paths for your feet," so that the lame may not be disabled, but rather healed.

When the Fathering Spirit comes back to the church, many who were lame *(crippled, unable to walk, struggling in their Christian life)* will be healed. The Fathering Spirit has a healing, resurrecting anointing. Mothers will want their children after the Fathering Spirit has ministered to them.

1 Kings 17:21 And he stretched himself upon the child three times, and cried unto the LORD, and said, O LORD my God, I pray thee, let this child's soul come into him again.

1 Kings 17:22 And the LORD heard the voice of Elijah; and the soul of the child came into him again, and he revived.

1 Kings 17:23 And Elijah took the child, and brought him down out of the chamber into the house, and delivered him unto his mother: and Elijah said, See, thy son liveth.

CHAPTER THREE

"The Goods of a Strong Man"

Mat. 12:28 But if I cast out devils by the Spirit of God, then the kingdom of God is come unto you.

Mat. 12:29 Or else how can one enter into a strong man's house, and spoil his goods, except he first bind the strong man? And then he will spoil his house.

Jesus says a (any) strong man must first be bound before his house can be robbed. Too many houses are being robbed because the strong men (the fathers) are being bound.

What are the "goods of a strong man?" His marriage, his wife and children, his job, his responsibility to his community, his purpose, and his destiny. A strong man is a mighty man, a powerful, boisterous man of much authority.

Luke 1:17 And he shall go before him in the spirit and power of Elias, to turn the hearts of the fathers to the children, and the disobedient to the wisdom of the just; to make ready a people prepared for the Lord.

Notice the Fathering Spirit has *power*, the spirit and power of Elijah to *turn* (convert) the hearts of the fathers back to their children and convert the hearts of the disobedient children to receive the wisdom of righteousness. Jesus says anyone who wishes to rob the strong man must first bind him. The Fathers are the strong men of their houses, protecting them from the wiles of the devil. Some of the wiles or strategies of the devil today are divorce, adultery, single-parent homes, increasing prison population, etc.

Luke 15:17 And when he came to himself, he said, How many hired servants of my father's have bread *enough and to spare, and I perish with hunger.*

Luke 15:18 I will arise and go to my father, and will say unto him, Father, I have sinned against heaven, and before thee,

Luke 15:19 And am no more worthy to be called thy son: make me as one of thy hired servants.

The prodigal son, as he is called, came to himself and realized that his father's servants were living better than he was because he let the enemy come into his father's house and steal him away and get him out of the strong man's house. Once the younger son was out of his father's (the strong man's) house, he had no power over poverty. He soon became broke and in need. When a son prematurely leaves his father's house, he becomes impoverished because he lacks the skills necessary to advance.

Luke 15:13 And not many days after the younger son gathered all together, and took his journey into a far country, and there wasted his substance with riotous living.

Luke 15:14 And when he had spent all, there arose a mighty famine in that land; and he began to be in want.

Notice that after he had spent or used up what his father had given him, a mighty famine hits the land. A mighty famine hit the land where ***he*** was, not where his father was. Whom can you depend on when a famine hits? Certainly, the strong man has prepared for the famine.

Luke 15:15 And he went and joined himself to a citizen of that country (he connected himself to a foreigner)*; and he sent him into his fields to feed swine.* Sent him into his fields? If there is a famine, there is nothing in the fields. So, the man just sent him out for nothing, into nothing, to do nothing.

The son who has left his father's house is now out there in a strange country trying to fulfill his destiny with no food, no shelter, no hope, and among stranger's who care nothing for him.

Luke 15:16 And he would fain have filled his belly with the husks that the swine did eat: and no man gave unto him.

His life is out of order and the ground will yield no fruit to him. The son went to his father and asked for his inheritance before it was time. *Eccl. 3:11 He hath made every thing beautiful in his time*: The enemy can only rob or take away those from their father's house who are impatient, undisciplined, or disloyal.

Gal. 4:1 Now I say, That the heir, as long as he is a child, differeth nothing from a servant, though he be lord of all;

Gal. 4:2 But is under tutors and governors until the time appointed of the father.

Timing is everything to the son whose father has built a godly heritage for him. God is a God of order and patterns; everything He does is based on patterns. Solomon says it this way: *Eccl. 1:9 The thing that hath been, it is that which shall be; and that which is done is that which shall be done: and there is no new thing under the sun.*

If we want to know what God desires, it's what He desired in the past. If we want to know what God is going to do, it's what He has done in the past. If we want to know what God is saying, it's what He has said in the past. What God desires to do, is what He did in the past. Specifically, God established Adam as the head of the household with his wife Eve and their children under them. From this pattern God would build His kingdom. In Ephesians chapter 5, Paul speaks of husbands loving their wives as Christ loves the church; he also speaks to wives to submit themselves to their husbands because Christ is the head of the church like the husband is the head of the family.

Then in Ephesians chapter 6, Paul tells the children to obey their parents in the Lord. Again, this is the pattern of the kingdom of God. God the Father, Israel as the mother (type), God the Son over the kingdom, and the church as the children of the (house) or kingdom. The first century church started in the homes of believers; there were no church buildings or any such edifices where the Body of Christ met. The synagogues were still very much as they are today, promoting Judaism. So the intact, in-order household was the model for the church and the kingdom of God.

When the house is out of order, the kingdom of God is greatly hindered. I believe this is why there has been such an attack not only on families, but also on the men who are to be husbands or fathers bringing their houses in order under the rulership of the Lord Jesus Christ.

Chapter Four

The Three Dimensions of Rulership

Rulership is the influencing, regulating, and governing of conduct. It means to guide and direct the affairs of others. A ruler is a straight piece of wood; therefore, rulership is the power to keep things straight.

Mat. 12:25. . . . Every kingdom divided against itself is brought to desolation; and every city or house divided against itself shall not stand:

Here we see plainly the three dimensions of rulership: the house, the city, and the kingdom.

Ruling from the House Level

The house is the quanta (the smallest measurement of a thing) of any organization. For example, there is a house within the house. The house I'm referring to is our spirit (which is made up of intuition, conscience, and communion) and our soul (mind, will, and emotions). Each spirit and soul is housed within a body; thus, a house within a house. Before born-again Christians can walk in true kingdom authority, they must take rulership over their house (spirit over body).

Jesus says in *Luke 21:19 In your patience* (endurance and consistency) *possess* (take charge of and control) *ye your souls.*

1 Th. 4:3 For this is the will of God, even your sanctification, that ye should abstain from fornication:

1 Th. 4:4 That every one of you should know how to possess his vessel in sanctification and honour;

It is God's will that every believer have rulership over his or her own house. Without having rulership over our houses, we would be easy prey for the devil. This is why drugs, alcohol, and other mind-altering substances are so demonic. They take away our rulership over the house God gave us.

When people live without self-rulership, they are out of control and society puts them in institutions to help them control themselves. If they can't stop robbing, killing, and hurting themselves or others, chances are they've lost the ability of self-rulership.

Prov. 25:28 He that hath no rule over his own spirit is like a city that is broken down, and without walls. There is no shelter or protection.

So, the house is put into a house, where the house is told when to wake up, when to eat, and when to sleep. There's no self-rulership of the house. This principle of self-rulership is so necessary that even Jesus had to go through it.

Mark 1:12 And immediately the Spirit driveth him into the wilderness.

Mark 1:13 And he was there in the wilderness forty days, tempted of Satan; and was with the wild beasts; and the angels ministered unto him.

Notice right after the Holy Ghost comes upon Jesus, the Bible says immediately the Holy Ghost drives Him into the wilderness to be tempted of the devil. Why? It would seem to me that the first thing Jesus would do is heal the sick or raise the dead. Before Jesus has the right to operate in the higher dimensions of rulership, He first has to deal with Himself! He has to deal with His own flesh, His own house. Before He can heal anybody else's house, He has to rule well His own house. The first question satan asks Jesus is about Him. *Mat. 4:3 And when the tempter came to him, he said, If thou be the Son of God, command that these stones be made bread.* Satan tries to see if Jesus will use His power for Himself.

The first question of rulership is: Can you handle personal power? What do you do with the power you now possess? What do you do with the time, money, and resources you have now? Abraham understood this principle. *Gen. 15:2 And Abram said, Lord GOD, what wilt thou give me, seeing I go childless, and the steward of my house is this Eliezer of Damascus? Gen. 15:3 And Abram said, Behold, to me thou hast given no seed: and, lo, one born in my house is mine heir.*

Abraham asked God, how can I be the father of many nations when my house is out of order? We need to understand the dimensions of rulership if we hope to win the world, because too many Christians are out of order.

1 Tim. 3:5 For if a man know not how to rule his own house, how shall he take care of the church of God?

Paul understood this perfectly. *2 Cor. 10:13 But we will not boast of things without our measure, but according to the measure of the rule which God hath distributed to us, a measure to reach even unto you.*

2 Cor. 10:14 For we stretch not ourselves beyond our measure . . .

In another place Paul says, *Eph. 4:7 But unto every one of us is given grace (God's divine ability) according to the measure of the gift of Christ.*

Eph. 4:13 Till we all come in the unity of the faith, and of the knowledge of the Son of God, unto a perfect man, unto the measure of the stature of the fullness of Christ:

Eph. 4:14 That we henceforth be no more children, tossed to and fro, and carried about with every wind of doctrine, by the sleight of men, and cunning craftiness, whereby they lie in wait to deceive;

Eph. 4:15 But speaking the truth in love, may grow up into him in all things, which is the head, even Christ:

This means that when we are truly united, the church will corporately function as a mature, full-grown Jesus in the earth. Not acting like spoiled children who all think they have it right and have more of Jesus than the other.

Eph. 4:16 From whom the whole body fitly joined together and compacted by that which every joint supplieth, according to the effectual working in the measure of every part, maketh increase of the body unto the edifying of itself in love.

When each part realizes and functions under its measure of rule, the church will not lack anything, but will grow and increase. Until then, we will continue to be weaker than we should, less blessed than we should be, and have less of an impact on cities and kingdoms in this world than we should.

Ruling at the City Level

Prov. 11:10 When it goeth well with the righteous, the city rejoiceth: and when the wicked perish, there is shouting.

Prov. 11:11 By the blessing of the upright the city is exalted: but it is overthrown by the mouth of the wicked.

Psa. 127:1 A Song of degrees for Solomon. Except the LORD build the house, they labour in vain that build it: except the LORD keep the city, the watchman waketh but in vain.

Gen. 18:32 And he said, Oh let not the Lord be angry, and I will speak yet but this once: Peradventure ten shall be found there. And he said, I will not destroy it for ten's sake.

God said He would not destroy the city for the 10's sake. There were 10 righteous people, which average out to be about two families. God said He would preserve Sodom and Gomorrah because of two righteous families. The number 10 symbolizes law, order, justice, truth, and completeness. The 10 commandments, the woman who had 10 coins, the 10 virgins, and there are 10 powers that cannot separate the believer from the love of God (Rom. 8:38).

Therefore, just 10 righteous people could change the condition of wicked Sodom and Gomorrah; just 10 righteous people who would stand up for righteousness. Again, we refer to our foundational scripture, when the righteous prospers in doing righteous deeds, the city rejoices or celebrates. By the blessing of the upright, the city is exalted; but when the wicked have the greater voice in the city, it is overthrown. A city is made righteous by righteous people. Righteous people are the result of the righteousness of God. The righteousness of God is only revealed through the gospel of Jesus Christ.

Rom. 1:16 For I am not ashamed of the gospel of Christ: for it is the power of God unto salvation to every one that believeth; to the Jew first, and also to the Greek.

Rom. 1:17 For therein is the righteousness of God revealed from faith to faith: as it is written, The just shall live by faith.

Luke 19:41 And when he was come near, he beheld the city, and wept over it,

Luke 19:42 Saying, If thou hadst known, even thou, at least in this thy day, the things which belong unto thy peace. but now they are hid from thine eyes.

Luke 19:43 For the days shall come upon thee, that thine enemies shall cast a trench about thee, and compass thee round, and keep thee in on every side,

Luke 19:44 And shall lay thee even with the ground, and thy children within thee; and they shall not leave in thee one stone upon another; because thou knewest not the time of thy visitation.

Luke 19:45 And he went into the temple, and began to cast out them that sold therein, and them that bought;

Luke 19:46 Saying unto them, It is written, My house is the house of prayer: but ye have made it a den of thieves.

Luke 19:47 And he taught daily in the temple. But the chief priests and the scribes and the chief of the people sought to destroy him.

The primary place the gospel is preached has traditionally been the church.

1 Pet. 4:17 For the time is come that judgment must begin at the house of God:

This is exactly what Jesus demonstrates in the scriptures. He weeps over the city (Jerusalem) saying that they missed their hour of visitation; the time of Jesus' ministry and entrance into the kingdom of God.

The city was so stubborn and religious that they could not discern that the scriptures that they had read for centuries had come to pass in Jesus, that He was the Christ.

Jesus knew the reason the city was in the condition it was in was because of the church (the house of God). He went into the temple and began teaching, but first, He drove out the moneychangers, those people who just went to church to prosper. Those people who only went to church out of obligation. They have no prayer life, they do not worship the Lord, and they have brought no sacrifice. The primary purpose of the moneychangers was to exchange animals for sacrifice to the people who came to the temple without a sacrifice. They sold the doves and exchanged foreign currency for Hebrew money to pay their temple tax (tithe).

Prov. 11:10 When it goeth well with the righteous, the city rejoiceth: and when the wicked perish, there is shouting.

Prov. 11:11 By the blessing of the upright the city is exalted: but it is overthrown by the mouth of the wicked.

Again, the righteous affect (bring change upon) the city. The problem is not that there are not enough righteous people; the problem has been that not enough righteous people have been blessing their cities with righteous deeds. In other words, if we desire to have a city that rejoices, the righteous have to build up their cities by doing righteous deeds in the city.

Acts 8:5 Then Philip went down to the city of Samaria, and preached Christ unto them.

Acts 8:6 And the people with one accord gave heed unto those things which Philip spake, hearing and seeing the miracles which he did.

Acts 8:7 For unclean spirits, crying with loud voice, came out of many that were possessed with them: and many taken with palsies, and that were lame, were healed.

Acts 8:8 And there was great joy in that city.

Notice the gospel is preached and followed by good deeds of miracles. The gospel is incomplete without the hearing and seeing of miracles; the deliverance and healing of the people so that great joy can come into the city.

Acts 17:1 Now when they had passed through Amphipolis and Apollonia, they came to Thessalonica, where was a synagogue of the Jews:

Acts 17:2 And Paul, as his manner was, went in unto them, and three sabbath days reasoned with them out of the scriptures,

Acts 17:5 Then the Jews became jealous. They attacked Jason's home and searched it for Paul and Silas in order to bring them out to the crowd.

Acts 17:6 And when they found them not, they drew Jason and certain brethren unto the rulers of the city, crying, ***These that have turned the world upside down are come hither also;***

Ruling at the Kingdom Level

Mark 4:36 And when they had sent away the multitude, they took him even as he was in the ship. And there were also with him other little ships.

Mark 4:37 And there arose a great storm of wind, and the waves beat into the ship, so that it was now full.

Mark 4:38 And he was in the hinder part of the ship, asleep on a pillow: and they awake him, and say unto him, Master, carest thou not that we perish?

Mark 4:39 And he arose, and rebuked the wind, and said unto the sea, Peace, be still. And the wind ceased, and there was a great calm.

Mark 4:40 And he said unto them, Why are ye so fearful? how is it that ye have no faith?

Mark 4:41 And they feared exceedingly, and said one to another, What manner of man is this, that even the wind and the sea obey him?

Rom. 13:1 Let every soul be subject unto the higher powers (authorities). For there is no power but of God: the powers that be are ordained (set up) of God. Rom. 13:2 Whosoever therefore resisteth the power, resisteth the (the order of God) ordinance of God:

How did Jesus come to such a place of authority? It was because He submitted Himself to God's order while here on earth. *Phil. 2:8 . . . became obedient unto death . . .* Jesus became something He never was, obedient. First, Jesus submitted to birth. That's right; He was born into the earth the same way everyone else is. *Mat. 2:1 Now when Jesus was born in Bethlehem of Judaea in the days of Herod the king . . .*

Second, He submitted Himself to His mother and father. *Luke 2:51 And he went down with them, and came to Nazareth, and was subject unto them: Deu. 5:16 Honour thy father and thy mother, as the LORD thy God hath commanded thee; that thy days may be prolonged, and that it may go well (have success, prosper) with thee, in the land which the LORD thy God giveth thee.*

Third, He submitted to spiritual authority, temptation from the devil, and John the Baptist. *Mat. 3:14 But John forbad him, saying, I have need to be baptized of thee, and comest thou to me? Mat. 3:15 And Jesus answering said unto him, Suffer it to be so now: for thus it becometh us to fulfil all righteousness. Jesus submitted to John the Baptist.*

Lastly, Jesus submitted Himself to the government of the day. *Mat. 17:24 And when they were come to Capernaum, they that received tribute money came to Peter, and said, Doth not your master pay tribute (taxes)?*

Mat. 17:25 He saith, Yes.

Mat. 17:27 Notwithstanding, lest we should offend them, go thou to the sea, and cast an hook, and take up the fish that first cometh up; and when thou hast opened his mouth, thou shalt find a piece of money: that take, and give unto them for me and thee.

Before Jesus could operate in kingdom authority, He had to submit Himself to the kingdoms of this world. Jesus did not fall from the sky; nor did He, as far as we know, fly through the sky. He was not covered with clouds or gold dust. No, He walked on the ground and He wore clothing as men do. He had to clean His teeth, comb His hair, and cook and eat food just like we do. In other words, Jesus voluntarily subjected himself to the kingdoms of this world.

Scientist have separated our physical world and divided it into kingdoms. The Animal Kingdom is the largest kingdom. It has more than 1 million named species. These species include the organisms that most people easily recognize as animals; human beings, deer, fish, insects, and snails. The Plant Kingdom consists of more than 260,000 known species. It includes those organisms that most people easily recognize as plants; magnolias, sunflowers, grasses, pine trees, ferns, and mosses. The Fungi Kingdom has more than 100,000 known species. These species include fungi, such as mushrooms and bread molds, as well as the lichens. The Protista Kingdom also has more than 100,000 known species. This kingdom includes green, golden, brown, and red algae; ciliates; sporozoans; sarcodines; and flagellates. The Prokaryotae Kingdom consists of bacteria, including blue-green algae or cyanobacteria. There are more than 10,000 known species in this kingdom. The Mineral Kingdom consists of minerals such as iron, copper, lead, zinc, gold, silver, and platinum. And of course, for those of us who are believers, we know there is also a Spiritual Kingdom. We have listed at least seven kingdoms with which man must interface or interact every single day of our lives.

Luke 10:17 And the seventy returned again with joy, saying, Lord, even the devils are subject unto us through thy name.

Jesus tells them not to be happy about ruling over the Spiritual Kingdom, but to be happy because their names are written in the lamb's book of life. In other words, it's because your names are in the lamb's book that you have this authority.

Mat. 6:33 But seek ye first the kingdom of God, and his righteousness; and all these things shall be added unto you. God's rule and righteousness.

This is why Jesus said to make the kingdom of God our priority, because every other kingdom is subject to it. It's the highest kingdom, and after entrance into God's kingdom everything else will be added. Remember the centurion, he understood authority. *Mat. 8:9 For I am a man under authority, having soldiers under me*: He understood that what made him a man of authority was the fact that he was under authority. Notice this is what he says first, he is under, so there are those under him.

Acts 8:27 And he arose and went: and, behold, a man of Ethiopia, an eunuch of great authority under Candace queen of the Ethiopians . . .

Luke 9:1 Then he called his twelve disciples together, and gave them power and authority over all devils, and to cure diseases.

Luke 9:2 And he sent them to preach the kingdom of God, and to heal the sick.

Luke 9:3 And he said unto them, Take nothing for your journey, neither staves, nor scrip, neither bread, neither money; neither have two coats apiece. Why, because with kingdom authority all these things will be added.

If a ministry consistently struggles in an effort to take care of its leaders, it is out of order.

1 Cor. 15:24 Then cometh the end, when he shall have delivered up the kingdom to God, even the Father; when he shall have put down all rule and all authority and power.

1 Cor. 15:25 For he must reign, till he hath put all enemies under his feet.

Mat. 12:28 But if I cast out devils by the Spirit of God, then the kingdom of God is come unto you.

Mat. 12:29 Or else how can one enter into a strong man's house, and spoil his goods, except he first bind the strong man? and then he will spoil his house.

Every born-again person is the strong man of his or her (physical) house.

Chapter Five

The Kingdom Anointing

Heb. 1:8 But unto the Son he saith, Thy throne, O God, is for ever and ever: a scepter of righteousness is the scepter of thy kingdom.

Heb. 1:9 Thou hast loved righteousness, and hated iniquity; therefore God, even thy God, hath anointed thee with the oil of gladness above thy fellows.

Notice what is said of Jesus Christ; *"Thy throne O God is forever and ever."* The throne represents rulership. Therefore, the rulership of Jesus Christ is forever. Why, because it's based upon righteousness. Its foundation is righteousness. For the very next words tell us that the scepter of His kingdom is righteousness. If we are going to rule at the kingdom level, we must understand the righteousness of God and how it applies to the life of the believer.

The scepter in scripture takes on two primary symbols. The first symbol of the scepter is that of kingly power and acceptance as with Esther and King Xerxes.

Those who approached the king without him extending his golden scepter toward them would be put to death.

The second symbol is that of David. In Psa. 2:9 the Bible says David will rule the nations with a rod (scepter) of iron and dash them to pieces like pottery. Here the scepter is clearly used as a weapon. #1 the scepter is a symbol of favor and acceptance to the kingdom citizen, #2 it's a symbol of correction and wrath outside the kingdom.

God demands righteousness; the next verse says Jesus loves righteousness. The word "love" here is the word "agapao," which means to breathe after, to love/desire unconditionally, to love to the point of sacrifice. We need to understand just how great God's need for righteousness is. It's not "phileo," God doesn't just have an affection for what's right. He absolutely lives for it, because He lives in it. There is no other place for God to live other than in righteousness. This is why the Father sent Jesus. He sacrificed Himself for the sake of righteousness because He loves it so much. God breathes after righteousness; He is uncompromising toward righteousness, and He will accept no substitute for it. The verse goes on to say that because Christ loves righteousness and hates iniquity, God has anointed him with the oil of gladness above others. The scripture says that "therefore" God has anointed thee. Through and by this act, or as a result of this attitude, God is able to anoint you above others. Anointed; smeared, rubbed on, to come into close contact with the very presence and essence of God's divine ability.

You see, as stated before, everyone from Moses to Jesus had to go through the process of house and city before they could rule at the kingdom level. Take Moses, for example, after he killed the Egyptian, he had to flee into the wilderness where he spent 40 years getting his house in order before he could go back and rule the city of Egypt with his rod. After he ruled the city, on his way to the kingdom level, he had some problems with the people who caused him to sin; or he failed to maintain an elevated state of righteousness, so he could not enter the Promised Land and rule at the kingdom level.

Whereas David got his house together in the cave of Adullam (which was his wilderness experience) and was eventually given the city of Ziklag. Once he ruled well at that level, he was anointed king of Judah (2 Samuel 2:4), David was never anointed king of Adullam or Ziklag; they were merely tests.

David was anointed by the prophet Samuel to be king over Israel, not king over a cave or king over a Philistine city. However, being anointed king over Israel enabled him to *rule* over the cave and the strange city because he was righteous, he had his house right. Before David was anointed King of Judah in Hebron, he had to conduct himself wisely in another anointed (mad) man's house, King Saul. Although King Saul was crazy, he was still the anointed king. David said touch not God's anointed, so David would not put his (mouth) hand on King Saul. David behaved himself righteously.

Luke 16:10 He that is faithful in that which is least is faithful also in much: and he that is unjust in the least is unjust also in much.

1 Sam. 22:1 David therefore departed thence, and escaped to the cave Adullam: and when his brethren and all his father's house heard it, they went down thither to him.

1 Sam. 22:2 And every one that was in distress, and every one that was in debt, and every one that was discontented, gathered themselves unto him; and he became a captain over them: and there were with him about four hundred men.

Most Christians would never take the job of ruling Adullam when they were anointed to be king of Israel. They would say, "God didn't show me Adullam, He showed me **all** of Israel and I ain't working in Adullam."

These 400 messed-up men became David's mighty men. This was David's first test of rulership/leadership. Could he turn these angry, broke, and confused men into mighty men of God? This is what qualified Him to rule Judah. It is not clear how long David and his men stayed in the cave Adullam, but if we read 1 Chr. 11:15 *(Now three of the thirty captains went down to the rock to David, into the cave of Adullam;),* we find that he stayed there long enough to turn at least 30 men into captains/leaders.

After King Saul was killed in battle, David asks God what he should do: 2 *Sam. 2:1 And it came to pass after this, that David inquired of the LORD, saying, Shall I go up into any of the cities of Judah? And the LORD said unto him, Go up. And David said, Whither shall I go up? And he said, Unto Hebron.*

2 Sam. 2:2 So David went up thither, and his two wives also, Ahinoam the Jezreelites, and Abigail Nabal's wife the Carmelite.

2 Sam. 2:3 And his men that were with him did David bring up, every man with his household: and they dwelt in the cities of Hebron.

2 Sam 2:4 And the men of Judah came, and there they anointed David king over the house of Judah.

2 Sam. 2:7 . . . and also the house of Judah have anointed me king over them. Notice the house (people) made David king.

The very next verses tell us that Abner made Ish-bosheth, Saul's son, king over Israel, but it only lasted for two years.

2 Sam. 2:11 And the time that David was king in Hebron over the house of Judah was seven years and six months. David used his kingly anointing to rule in a cave, Ziklag (a strange city) and then Judah for 7 years, but not yet the whole kingdom

2 Sam. 5:2 NCV Even when Saul was king, you were the one who led Israel in battle. The LORD said to you, 'You will be a shepherd for my people Israel. You will be their leader.'

2 Sam. 5:3 So all the older leaders of Israel came to King David at Hebron, and he made an agreement with them in Hebron in the presence of the LORD. Then they poured oil on David to make him king over Israel.

2 Sam. 5:4 David was thirty years old when he became king, and he ruled forty years.

2 Sam. 5:5 He was king over Judah in Hebron for seven years and six months, and he was king over all Israel and Judah in Jerusalem for thirty-three years.

Notice also that again the heads of the families came and anointed David King over Israel. The first anointing came from the prophet; the last two came from the people in the presence of God.

Because David waited on the LORD and did it right, his rulership lasted longer and was stronger than those who anointed/appointed themselves. First God established the house of David, then God established the city of David, and ultimately God established the Kingdom of David!

Psa. 127:1 Except the LORD build the house, they labour in vain that build it: except the LORD keep the city, the watchman waketh but in vain.

There is no sense in talking kingdom when there are no cities or houses to rule. You see, it's during the wilderness time that we learn the presence of God so we can take it into the city. *2 Sam. 6:12 So David went and brought up the ark of God from the house of Obededom into the city of David with gladness.*

After bringing the Ark into the city of David, the presence of God established the kingdom of David. Of course, we know that as a result of David's sin with Bathsheba, he lost rulership over his own house and the (earthly) kingdom was eventually divided.

2 Sam. 12:10 Now therefore the sword shall never depart from thine house; because thou hast despised me, and hast taken the wife of Uriah the Hittite to be thy wife.

2 Sam. 12:11 Thus saith the LORD, Behold, I will raise up evil against thee out of thine own house, and I will take thy wives before thine eyes, and give them unto thy neighbour, and he shall lie with thy wives in the sight of this sun.

So, here we see the principle of house, city, and kingdom played out in scripture through the life of King David. When God establishes His kingdom through David, David still had to maintain his house; because the house is the foundation of the city and the kingdom. Once David brought disorder to his house, it eventually affected his kingdom. When the enemy attacks the house, he's really after your authority and rulership, your kingdom.

Mat. 12:25 . . . Every kingdom divided against itself is brought to desolation; and every city or house divided against itself shall not stand:

Therefore, we are right back where we started, at the house level, which is where the battle never ends. *Luke 1:17 And he shall go before him in the spirit and power of Elias, to turn the hearts of the fathers to the children, and the disobedient to the wisdom of the just; to make ready a people prepared for the Lord.* This is why in the last days, the Fathering Spirit is what is going to prepare the church for the authority of Jesus. Notice Luke calls him Lord, "kurios" in the Greek. It means authority, master, controller, and ruler. There can be no kingdom to rule unless there are houses being ruled by godly fathers in cities ruled by righteous men who make up a righteous kingdom.

Luke 1:17 . . . to make ready a people prepared for the Lord. It's the Fathering Spirit that gets the people ready for the kingdom. Jesus isn't coming back to a church service, a conference, or a denomination. He's coming back for a kingdom already set in order for Him to rule.

Rev. 11:15 . . . The kingdoms of this world are become the kingdoms of our Lord, and of his Christ; and he shall reign forever and ever.

1 Cor. 15:28 But when God puts everything under Christ's authority, the Son will put himself under God's authority, since God had put everything under the Son's authority. Then God will have rule over everything.

Then God the Father will have His house in order. When our houses submit to the household of faith, Jesus is Lord, and when Jesus is Lord, he will turn everything over to the father in order.

CHAPTER SIX

Dividing the House

Luke 15:11 And he said, A certain man had two sons:

Luke 15:12 And the younger of them said to his father, Father, give me the portion of goods that falleth to me. And he divided unto them his living.

Luke 15:13 And not many days after the younger son gathered all together, and took his journey into a far country, and there wasted his substance with riotous living.

Luke 15:14 And when he had spent all, there arose a mighty famine in that land; and he began to be in want.

The younger son wanted his inheritance now, before it was time. He was immature and the time was premature. Jewish law stated that at the time of the fathers death one-third of the estate belonged to the younger and two-thirds to the elder (Deut. 21:17). Because the younger son wanted his share while the father lived, the father not only had to give the younger son his share, but he had to give the elder son his share as well. This means the younger son got one-third and the elder son got two-thirds.

We cannot overlook some obvious similarities in history here. One is the fact that the younger son took one-third of his father's goods, just as Lucifer took one-third of the Father's angels in heaven. This is nothing but the spirit of division. There are many truths to be revealed here in this story. Another fact that cannot be overlooked is that in giving the son one-third of the estate, the father's house is automatically weakened. However, the father doesn't stop there. He also gives the eldest his portion.

What then does the father possess? What is left for him? Since he is gracious enough to give his sons their inheritance, now he has nothing but a title, father. The younger son asks for the goods as if the father owed it to him. Just as Lucifer or satan did in Rev. 12:4, Ezk 28, and Isaiah 14. He seeks to weaken the house of God through division.

Gal. 4:1 Now I say, That the heir, as long as he is a child, differeth nothing from a servant, though he be lord of all;

Gal. 4:2 But is under tutors and governors until the time appointed of the father.

Notice that the time of release is established by the father, not the son. The son has not been given the right to say when it is time for him to receive his inheritance; but is under tutors and governors until the father decides. The tutors and governors are designed to assist the father with oversight and discipline. One of the meanings of the Hebrew word son is "built by," because the son always builds upon what his father has left him. This is another reason why a good (father) man leaves an inheritance for his children's children. In order for the son to build upon the father's work, he must see his father's work as valuable. He must guard and protect it with his very life because the enemy is out to destroy the father's legacy. He wants the sons to have to begin again, to start over.

Remember, Jesus says anyone who wishes to rob the strong man must first bind him. The son can finish or at least accomplish more than his father did, and so it is with the next generations. Sons are builders, but if they have not been left with at least the blueprints, what can they build? Each generation is responsible for the next. This great enterprise the Lord is building takes men of vision, men of character, and men of strength. Men who understand the power of the Fathering Spirit and who realize that God wants to do something that out lasts their personal ministries, that the greatest hope of achieving world evangelism is by fathering sons who will do greater works than they. By turning the hearts of the sons back to the Father in heaven, so His holy will can be done on earth as it is in heaven.

Author Contact Information

For more information and pricing, please contact the church office at:

Christian Faith Fellowship Church
1727 27th Street
Zion, IL 60099
Phone: 847.731.0700
Fax: 847.731.1765
Email: cffc@ameritech.net
Web site: www.cffczion.org

Audio Tapes/CDs by Apostle E. James Logan

Series

School of Prayer

School of Prophets

Angels

Trusting God

The Spiritual Mind

Vision Series

Truth, Righteousness and the Glory of God

Death Series

Hearing the Voice of God

Walking in the Spirit

Serving the Lord

Lord Teach Us To Pray

Individual Messages

5 Reasons Why I'm a Christian

A Faith That Works

A Message: Being

A New Commandment

And He Restores My Soul

And Jesus Said Come

Angels I

Angels II

Angels III

Angels IV

Big Faith vs. Little Faith

Breaking the Spirit of Fear

But for the Glory of God

By Faith

Can Anything Good Come From This II?

Celebration of Praise

Coming Through

Controlling Your Own Breath

Death of the Body-Only a Transition

Death: A Necessary Stage of Transformation I

Death: A Necessary Stage of Transformation II

Defeating Oppression

Discerning of Spirits

Discipleship and Soul Winning

Divine Logic

Early I Will Seek Thee

Evidence of the Resurrection

Faith in the Divine Logic of God

Fellowship With the Lamb

Fight The Good Fight of Faith

Get Ready for Something New

Getting Results From The Word That You Hear

God Expects Us to Love Him

God's About to Show Me Off

God's Favor on Your Life

God's Love Bestowed On Us

Going Into Maturity

Having a Clear Understanding (2 tapes)

Having a Heart for the Lost

Hearing the Voice of God I

Hearing the Voice of God II

Honoring God I

Honoring God II

How to Get Your Prayers Answered

How to Accomplish the Will of God

How to Enter Into God's Rest (2 tapes)

How to Gain Eternal Life

How to Keep What You Have and Get More

I am Going for It

Interrupted Plans

It's Time for Your Come Back

It's Time to Build the Kingdom

It's Time to Release the Anointing On Your Life

Just Before Your Breakthrough

Keys to the Kingdom: Meditation

Kingdom Keys

Kingdom Mentality I: From Glory to Glory

Kingdom Mentality II

Laborers of Love

Let's Get Serious

Life Isn't Fair, So Use Your Faith

Lord Teach Us to Pray I

Lord Teach Us to Pray II

Lord Teach Us to Pray III

Marriage and Divorce

Marriage Seminar

My Destiny is Greater Than My Pain

No Lack

No Penalty No Pain

No Reputation

Not By Might Nor By Power

Oppression

Overwhelmed by His Presence

People Ready for War

Perfection: The Condition of the Heart

Pride: The Unity Killer

Productiveness

Prophecy and Prophets

Prophetic Word of Authority

Prove Me Saith the Lord

Releasing the power of God Through Unity

Remedies for the Time

School of Prayer (7 CD Set)

School of Prophets (12 CD Set)

Seasons

Seeing Into the Heavenly Realm

Serving God I

Serving God pt II

Serving the Lord

Skill for Living

Stabilize Your Life

Stewardship

Suffering and the Christian

Taking Your Authority

The Act of Receiving I

The Act of Receiving II

The Act of Receiving III

The Actions of Mature Believers

The Blessings of Abraham

The Body of Christ I

The Body of Christ II

The Body of Sin

The Christian Life: A Life of Sacrifice

The Divine Order of Love

The Flow of the Spirit

The Four Women of Revelation-Israel

The Four Women of Revelations

The Four Women of Revelation-The Bride

The Four Women of Revelation-The Great Whore

The Gift of the Holy Spirit I

The Gift of the Holy Spirit II

The God Identity (2 tapes)

The Goodness of God

The Greatest of All graces

The Hand of God

The Holy Ghost

The Holy Kiss

The Last Person You Would Expect

The Last Straw (2 tapes)

The Lord Will See To It

The Love of God Towards Us

The Making of a Disciple I

The Making of a Disciple II

The Manifestation of the Sons of God

The Mercy of God

The Ministry Function of The Church

The Path of the Righteous

The Pleasure of God

The Pleasures of Sin

The Posture of a Worshipper

The Power is Here

The Power of Prophecy

The Power of Righteousness I

The Power of Righteousness II

The Power of Righteousness III

The Power of Righteousness IV

The Power of the Church of Jesus Christ

The Power of the Holy Ghost

The Power of Thoughts

The Power to Overcome

The Practice of Godliness I and II

The Practice of Godliness III

The Practice of Godliness IV

The Prelude to a Miracle

The Presence of the Lord

The Prophetic Gift

The Ransom

The Same Jesus

The Servant of God (2 tapes)

The Silence of the Lambs

The Spiritual Mind

The Spiritual Mind II

The Three Levels of Communion

The Value of Our Faith

The Vocal Gift

The Wages of Sin

The Weakness of God

The Windows of Heaven

The Winds of Change

The Wrath of God

This Kind

True Love For God

True Overcomers/True Sons of God

Trusting God I

Trusting God II

Truth, Righteousness, and the Glory of God I

Truth, Righteousness, and the Glory of God II

Union With Christ

Unity

Unmarried Seminar

Victory Over the Flesh

Vision Produces Unity I

Vision Produces Unity II

Vision: The Discipleship of Following

Vision: The Discipline of Following

Vision: The Power of Discipline

Vision: The Power of Hope

Vision: The Power of Vision

Vision: Trusting and Following God

Vision: What You See is What You Get I

Vision: What You See is What You Get II

Walking in the Spirit I

Walking in the Spirit II

Wash, Cleanse, and Purge

We're Leaving Here Together

What is Sin?

When Will You Come To Me?

Who's At Your Door?

Why Jesus Came

Why We Should Pray

You Grow From What You Know

You've Been Shifted

Apostle E. James Logan is the Senior Pastor of Christian Faith Fellowship Church in Zion, Illinois. He is committed to building the Body of Christ in the unity of the Spirit and the bond of peace. James Logan possesses the unique ability to uncover God's purpose in the lives of people often shrouded by the pain of the past and the snares of the enemy.

You will be blessed as you receive from this man of God called, chosen, and anointed for these last days. May your destiny become clearer than ever as God reveals more of Himself to you through His servant.

Christian Faith Fellowship Church
1727 27th Street Zion, IL 60099
847.731.0700

Notes

Notes

Notes

Notes

Notes

Notes

Notes

Notes

Notes

Notes

Notes

www.ingramcontent.com/pod-product-compliance
Lightning Source LLC
Chambersburg PA
CBHW032013040426
42448CB00006B/615

* 9 7 8 1 9 3 2 5 0 3 5 2 4 *